Bible Study Series
for senior high

WHY
Spiritual
Growth
MATTERS

Group

Loveland, Colorado

Why Spiritual Growth Matters

Core Belief Bible Study Series

Copyright © 1997 Group Publishing, Inc.

Credits

Editor: Karl Leuthauser
Creative Development Editor: Paul Woods
Chief Creative Officer: Joani Schultz
Copy Editor: Pamela Shoup
Art Director: Bill Fisher
Computer Graphic Artist: Ray Tollison
Photographer: Craig DeMartino
Production Manager: Gingar Kunkel

ISBN 0-7644-0884-4
10 9 8 7 6 5 4 3 2   06 05 04 03 02 01 00 99

Printed in the United States of America.

Bible Study Series
for senior high

contents:

the ▼Studies

▼Spiritual Growth as a
Core Christian Belief

Teenagers today are very discerning. They're not easily fooled by people who put on spiritual fronts but have little spiritual depth. Unfortunately, teenagers often see people like that in churches today—people who may very well have a true faith in Jesus, but who aren't really growing closer to God in their daily lives. Seeing such stagnant Christians can turn kids off to a vital, growing relationship with God.

By understanding the true nature of spiritual growth, your kids can see that a stagnant or hypocritical relationship with God isn't what God wants. Instead, kids can see that God desires a growing, deepening relationship with his children that's exciting and life-changing. Once kids know what's possible with God, they'll be motivated to seek him with all their hearts.

The studies in this book will challenge your kids to strive for genuine growth in their faith. While participating in the first study, kids will compare counterfeit growth with true spiritual growth by discussing the **New Age movement.** Your students will have the opportunity to discover that spiritual growth isn't concerned with human potential or greatness but is a result of God working in us to make us more like the Lord Jesus Christ.

The second and third studies are designed to help your kids understand sexuality and gender roles. The second study will help your young men discover what it means to be a "real" man as they learn about **masculinity.** The third study will help girls understand their identity as women of God as they attempt to define **femininity.** Your young men and women will have the opportunity to learn that in the maze of pressures from society, only God can make them the men and women they're created to be.

In the fourth study, kids will learn that they aren't alone on their quest for spiritual growth. You will help kids understand that it takes the **accountability** of family and friends to help them focus and grow in their roles as Christians.

The final study will help kids investigate a very important but not often addressed aspect of spiritual growth. By looking at what being **childlike** really means, they can find that in the midst of a hectic and crazy world, their faith and trust in God can be simple, consistent, and growing.

Becoming a Christian marks the beginning of a miraculous change that continues to progress right up to the moment of death, and beyond. God never intended teenagers to trust in Jesus for their salvation, then live out the rest of their lives without God. He wants them to grow in their relationship with him—personally experiencing the grace, mercy and love of God in ever-increasing measures every day.

For a more comprehensive look at this Core Christian Belief, read Group's **Get Real: Making Core Christian Beliefs Relevant to Teenagers.**

DEPTHFINDER
HOW THE BIBLE DESCRIBES SPIRITUAL GROWTH

Spiritual growth is a process. Although you become a "new creation" in Christ at the moment you believe in him, that doesn't mean that you're automatically freed from the tendency to sin. In fact, any Christian who's striving to live for Christ will struggle with the desire to sin. But through the power cf the Holy Spirit you can say no to sin.

Over time, as you continue to choose God's way, you'll become more and more like Jesus. How that growth takes place is a combination of the Holy Spirit's leading in your life and your conscious decision to follow that leading instead of your sinful desires.

According to Scripture, spiritual growth occurs as we grow in knowledge, holiness, and intimacy with God (John 14:26; 16:13-14; Romans 7:14-25; 8:5-16, 22-27; 2 Corinthians 5:17; Galatians 5:16-25; 6:8; 1 John 3:21-24). Let's take a closer look at each of these aspects:

- **Spiritual growth means growing in knowledge.** Before we can make changes in our lives, we have to know what God wants for us. That knowledge comes largely through the study of the Bible. By reading and studying the Bible, as well as other books and materials that are based on biblical principles, we can learn more about God and how he wants us to live. In the same way, we can learn from other Christians and the leading of the Holy Spirit in our lives. Although growing in knowledge is a part of spiritual growth, gaining knowledge alone will not result in spiritual growth (Deuteronomy 5:1; Mark 12:24; John 5:39-40; Philippians 1:9-11; 2 Timothy 2:15; 3:14-17).

- **Spiritual growth means growing in holiness before God.** Holiness involves striving to follow the example of Christ in all that we do. Acting on what we learn about God shows that we really know and love him. And obeying God's leading is true spiritual growth—producing the fruit of the Spirit in our lives (Psalm 1:1-2; 119:97-104; Galatians 5:22-23; Ephesians 1:17; 5:1-2; 1 John 2:3-6; 2 Timothy 3:14-17; James 4:4-8).

- **Spiritual growth means becoming like Jesus in the way we treat other Christians.** God doesn't intend for us to function in this world as loner Christians. In the church he gave us brothers and sisters to share our hurts and needs as we struggle to grow through the difficulties of life. Part of that growth involves learning to use the spiritual gifts God gives us through the Holy Spirit. Those gifts are given to Christians to be used for the benefit of the church and those outside the church as well (1 Corinthians 12:1-31; Galatians 6:1-5; 1 Thessalonians 5:11; 2 Thessalonians 1:3-4; Hebrews 10:24-25; James 5:13-20).

- **Spiritual growth means becoming like Jesus in the way we live in the world.** Once we become Christians, we're no longer to love the world, but we're to love the people in the world. God wants us to care for the poor, the sick, the orphans, the widows, and all those who don't have a relationship with him through Jesus. He wants us to serve him by serving them. He also wants us to let others know how they can have the relationship with him that we do. As we grow in our understanding of who God is and what he has done for us, we will grow in compassion for the hurting people God loves (Proverbs 14:21; Matthew 14:14; 19:21; 25:34-40; 28:19-20; Mark 6:34; Luke 15:11-32; James 1:27; 1 Peter 3:15).

CORE CHRISTIAN BELIEF OVERVIEW

Here are the twenty-four Core Christian Belief categories that form the backbone of Core Belief Bible Study Series:

The Nature of God	Jesus Christ	The Holy Spirit
Humanity	Evil	Suffering
Creation	The Spiritual Realm	The Bible
Salvation	Spiritual Growth	Personal Character
God's Justice	Sin & Forgiveness	The Last Days
Love	The Church	Worship
Authority	Prayer	Family
Service	Relationships	Sharing Faith

Look for Group's Core Belief Bible Study Series books in these other Core Christian Beliefs!

about

Bible Study Series
for senior high

Think for a moment about your young people. When your students walk out of your youth program after they graduate from junior high or high school, what do you want them to know? What foundation do you want them to have so they can make wise choices?

You probably want them to know the essentials of the Christian faith. You want them to base everything they do on the foundational truths of Christianity. Are you meeting this goal?

If you have any doubt that your kids will walk into adulthood knowing and living by the tenets of the Christian faith, then you've picked up the right book. All the books in Group's Core Belief Bible Study Series encourage young people to discover the essentials of Christianity and to put those essentials into practice. Let us explain...

What Is Group's Core Belief Bible Study Series?

Group's Core Belief Bible Study Series is a biblically in-depth study series for junior high and senior high teenagers. This Bible study series utilizes four defining commitments to create each study. These "plumb lines" provide structure and continuity for every activity, study, project, and discussion. They are:

● **A Commitment to Biblical Depth**—Core Belief Bible Study Series is founded on the belief that kids not only *can* understand the deeper truths of the Bible but also *want* to understand them. Therefore, the activities and studies in this series strive to explain the "why" behind every truth we explore. That way, kids learn principles, not just rules.

● **A Commitment to Relevance**—Most kids aren't interested in abstract theories or doctrines about the universe. They want to know how to live successfully right now, today, in the heat of problems they can't ignore. Because of this, each study connects a real-life need with biblical principles that speak directly to that need. This study series finally bridges the gap between Bible truths and the real-world issues kids face.

● **A Commitment to Variety**—Today's young people have been raised in a sound bite world. They demand variety. For that reason, no two meetings in this study series are shaped exactly the same.

● **A Commitment to Active and Interactive Learning**—Active learning is learning by doing. Interactive learning simply takes active learning a step further by having kids teach each other what they've learned. It's a process that helps kids internalize and remember their discoveries.

For a more detailed description of these concepts, see the section titled "Why Active and Interactive Learning Works With Teenagers" beginning on page 57.

So how can you accomplish all this in a set of four easy-to-lead Bible studies? By weaving together various "power" elements to produce a fun experience that leaves kids challenged and encouraged.

Turn the page to take a look at some of the power elements used in this series.

Betrayed!

HELPING KIDS DEAL WITH REJECTION FROM THE PEOPLE THEY LOVE

by Jennifer Carrell

THE POINT:

God is love.

■ Betrayal has very little shock value for this generation. It's as commonplace as compact discs and mosh pits. For many kids today, betrayal characterizes their parents' wedding vows. It's part of their curriculum at school; it defines the headlines and evening news. Betrayal is not only accepted—it's expected. ■ At the heart of such acceptance lies the belief that nothing is absolute. No vow, no law, no promise can be trusted. Relationships are betrayed at the earliest convenience. Repeatedly, kids see that something called "love" lasts just as long as it's ... permanence. But deep inside, they hunger to see a

The Study
AT A GLANCE

SECTION	MINUTES	WHAT STUDENTS WILL DO	SUPPLIES
Discussion Starter	up to 5	JUMP-START—Identify some of the most common themes in today's movies.	Newsprint, marker
Investigation of Betrayal	12 to 15	REALITY CHECK—Form groups to compare anonymous, real-life stories of betrayal with experiences in their own lives.	"Profiles of Betrayal" handouts (p. 20), highlighter pens, newsprint, marker, tape
	3 to 5	WHO BETRAYED WHOM?—Guess the identities of the people profiled in the handouts.	Paper, tape, pen
Investigation of True Love	15 to 18	SOURCE WORK—Study and discuss God's definition of perfect love.	Bibles, newsprint, marker
	5 to 7	LOVE MESSAGES—Create unique ways to send a "message of love" to the victims of betrayal they've been studying.	Newsprint, markers, tape
Personal Application	10 to 15	SYMBOLIC LOVE—Give a partner a personal symbol of perfect love.	Paper lunch sack, pens, scissors, paper, catalogs

notes:

● **A Relevant Topic**—More than ever before, kids live in the now. What matters to them and what attracts their hearts is what's happening in their world at this moment. For this reason, every Core Belief Bible Study focuses on a particular hot topic that kids care about.

● **A Core Christian Belief**—Group's Core Belief Bible Study Series organizes the wealth of Christian truth and experience into twenty-four Core Christian Belief categories. These twenty-four headings act as umbrellas for a collection of detailed beliefs that define Christianity and set it apart from the world and every other religion. Each book in this series features one Core Christian Belief with lessons suited for junior high or senior high students.

"But," you ask, "won't my kids be bored talking about all these spiritual beliefs?" No way! As a youth leader, you know the value of using hot topics to connect with young people. Ultimately teenagers talk about issues because they're searching for meaning in their lives. They want to find the one equation that will make sense of all the confusing events happening around them. Each Core Belief Bible Study answers that need by connecting a hot topic with a powerful Christian principle. Kids walk away from the study with something more solid than just the shifting ebb and flow of their own opinions. They walk away with a deeper understanding of their Christian faith.

● **The Point**—This simple statement is designed to be the intersection between the Core Christian Belief and the hot topic. Everything in the study ultimately focuses on The Point so that kids study it and allow it time to sink into their hearts.

● **The Study at a Glance**—A quick look at this chart will tell you what kids will do, how long it will take them to do it, and what supplies you'll need to get it done.

The Bible Connection—This is the power base of each study. Whether it's just one verse or several chapters, The Bible Connection provides the vital link between kids' minds and their hearts. The content of each Core Belief Bible Study reflects the belief that the true power of God—the power to expose, heal, and change kids' lives—is contained in his Word.

THE POINT OF *BETRAYED!*:

God is love.

THE BIBLE CONNECTION

1 JOHN 4:7-21 The Apostle John explains the nature and definition of perfect love.

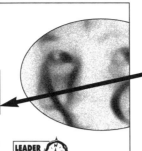

In this study, kids will compare the imperfect love defined in real-life stories of betrayal to God's definition of perfect love.

By making this comparison, kids can discover that God is love and therefore incapable of betraying them. Then they'll be able to recognize the incredible opportunity God offers to experience the only relationship worthy of their absolute trust.

Explore the verses in The Bible Connect mation in the Depthfinder boxes throughou understanding of how these Scriptures con

LEADER TIP for The Study

THE STUDY

DISCUSSION STARTER ▼

Jump-Start (up to 5 minutes) As kids arrive, ask them to thi common themes in movies, books, TV sho have kids each contribute ideas for a mas two other kids in the room and sharing sider providing copies of People magazine t what's currently showing on television or at their suggestions, write their responses on n **come up with a lot of great ideas. Even th ent, look through this list and try to disc ments most of these themes have in com**

After kids make several suggestions, menti responses are connected with the idea of bet

● **Why do you think betrayal is such a**

Betrayed! **17**

LEADER TIP for The Study

Because this topic can be so powerful and relevant to kids' lives, your group members may be tempted to get caught up in issues and lose sight of the deeper biblical principle found in The Point. Help your kids grasp The Point by guiding kids to focus on the biblical investigation and discussing how God's truth connects with reality in their lives.

DEPTHFINDER UNDERSTANDING INTEGRITY

Your students may not be entirely familiar with the meaning of integrity, especially as it might apply to God's character in the Trinity. Use these definitions (taken from Webster's II New Riverside Dictionary) and other information to help you guide kids toward a better understanding of how God maintains integrity through the three expressions of the Trinity.

Integrity: 1. Firm adherence to a code or standard of values. 2. The state of being unimpaired. 3. The quality or condition of being undivided.

Synonyms for integrity include probity, completeness, wholeness, soundness, and perfection.

Our word "integrity" comes from the Latin word *integritas*, which means soundness. *Integritas* is also the root of the word "integer," which means "whole or complete," as in a "whole" number.

The Hebrew word that's often translated "integrity" (for example, in Psalm 25:21 [NIV]) is *tam*. It means whole, perfect, sincere, and honest.

CREATIVE GOD-EXPLORATION ▼

Top Hats (18 to 20 minutes) Form three groups, with each trio member from the previous activity going to a different group. Give each group Bibles, paper, and pens, and assign each group a different hat God wears: Father, Son, or Holy Spirit.

Depthfinder Boxes—These informative sidelights located throughout each study add insight into a particular passage, word, historical fact, or Christian doctrine. Depthfinder boxes also provide insight into teen culture, adolescent development, current events, and philosophy.

Leader Tips—These handy information boxes coach you through the study, offering helpful suggestions on everything from altering activities for different-sized groups to streamlining discussions to using effective discipline techniques.

Holy Profiles

Your assigned Bible passage describes how a particular person or group responded when confronted with God's holiness. Use the information in your passage to help your group discuss the questions below. Then use your flashlights to teach the other two groups what you discover.

■ Based on your passage, what does holiness look like?

■ What does holiness sound like?

■ When people see God's holiness, how does it affect them?

■ How is this response to God's holiness like humility?

■ Based on your passage, how would you describe humility?

■ Why is humility an appropriate human response to God's holiness?

■ Based on what you see in your passage, do you think you are a humble person? Why or why not?

■ What's one way you could develop humility in your life this week?

Handouts—Most Core Belief Bible Studies include photocopiable handouts to use with your group. Handouts might take the form of a fun game, a lively discussion starter, or a challenging study page for kids to take home—anything to make your study more meaningful and effective.

The Last Word on Core Belief Bible Studies

Soon after you begin to use Group's Core Belief Bible Study Series, you'll see signs of real growth in your group members. Your kids will gain a deeper understanding of the Bible and of their own Christian faith. They'll see more clearly how a relationship with Jesus affects their daily lives. And they'll grow closer to God.

But that's not all. You'll also see kids grow closer to one another.

That's because this series is founded on the principle that Christian faith grows best in the context of relationship. Each study uses a variety of interactive pairs and small groups and always includes discussion questions that promote deeper relationships. The friendships kids will build through this study series will enable them to grow *together* toward a deeper relationship with God.

To Be God...
or Godly

The Quest for True Spirituality

Spiritual growth means becoming more like Jesus.

■ Did you know...67 percent of American adults claim to have psychic experiences?...42 percent of American adults believe they've been in contact with someone who has died?...31 percent believe that some people have magical powers?...30 million Americans (about one in four) believe in reincarnation? ■ These statistics are from the book *Understanding the New Age* by Russell Chandler. According to Chandler, a former religion writer for the Los Angeles Times, the New Age movement is probably the most widespread, powerful phenomenon affecting our culture today. ■ Need more than stats to convince you? Just ask your group members what they think about the beliefs described above. ■ Their responses may surprise you. ■ This study contrasts the New Age approach to spirituality with the true spiritual growth described in the Bible, and helps kids discover that true spirituality doesn't come from a séance or an out-of-body experience. ■ It comes from Jesus.

The Study
AT A GLANCE

SECTION	MINUTES	WHAT STUDENTS WILL DO	SUPPLIES
Creative Comparison	5 to 10	TRUE OR FALSE?—Contrast New Age "spirituality" with the spirituality depicted in Psalm 1.	Bibles, tea-light candles, matchbooks, one large candle, "True or False Spirituality" Depthfinder quotes (p. 18)
Spiritual Exploration	25 to 30	CHANGING FACES—Remake each other into the image of someone they admire.	Bibles, paper, masking tape, yarn, assorted nonpermanent markers
Personal Evaluation	10 to 15	JESUS AND ME—Privately explore ways they can get to know Jesus better in the coming weeks.	Large candle, tea-light candles, "Jesus and Me" handouts (p. 22), pencils, newsprint, tape, markers
Group Building	5 to 10	JESUS AND YOU—Tell which Christlike qualities they see in each other.	Tea-light candles

notes:

THE POINT OF *TO BE GOD... OR GODLY:*

Spiritual growth means becoming more like Jesus.

THE BIBLE CONNECTION

| PSALM 1 | The psalmist describes godly spirituality. |
| GALATIANS 5:22-23 | Paul lists the fruit that comes from true spirituality. |

I n this study, kids will experience a personal encounter with God to help them discover their own true "spirituality" in the light of their Christian faith.

Through this experience, your kids will learn to recognize the false spirituality offered by the New Age movement and discover that becoming more intimate with Jesus Christ is the key to real spiritual growth.

Explore the verses in The Bible Connection, then examine the information in the Depthfinder boxes throughout the study to gain a deeper understanding of how these Scriptures connect with your young people.

LEADER TIP for The Study

Because this topic can be so powerful and relevant to kids' lives, your group members may be tempted to get caught up in issues and lose sight of the deeper biblical principle found in The Point. Help your kids grasp The Point by guiding kids to focus on the biblical investigation and discussing how God's truth connects with reality in their lives.

THE STUDY

CREATIVE COMPARISON ▼

True or False? (5 to 10 minutes) Form a circle of chairs, and place one chair in the center. Once kids arrive, ask for four volunteers, and give each a tea-light candle, a matchbook, and a photocopy of one quote from the "True or False Spirituality" Depthfinder (p. 18). Keep one large candle next to you.

Turn off the room lights, then have the four volunteers light their candles one at a time and read aloud the quotes you provided. When

DEPTHFINDER   TRUE OR FALSE SPIRITUALITY

The New Age movement is a loosely connected assortment of beliefs about the nature of life, humanity, and eternity. Although the beliefs often seem to contradict each other, they all share a common "root" belief: that humans are capable of attaining "godhood" or are, in fact, already "gods." Here's a sampling of some of those New Age beliefs, as explained in *The Seduction of Our Children*, by Neil T. Anderson and Steve Russo:

1. This is what it means to be spiritual: *God is everything, and everything is God.* Everything in creation—trees, snails, books, people, earthworms—are one divine essence. The more we are attuned to that consciousness, the more we are God.

2. This is what it means to be spiritual: *We must become cosmically conscious.* We become self-realized through reincarnation, where our souls progress through many life cycles until we become fully conscious of the universe.

3. This is what it means to be spiritual: *We must work together toward the harmony of a one-world government.* A new global civilization and a mystic world religion is necessary to unite all people in a worldwide consciousness and create world peace.

4. This is what it means to be spiritual: *What you believe to be good is good, and what you believe to be evil is evil.* Reality is what you make it. By changing what you believe, you can change reality.

they finish, light the large candle and read aloud Psalm 1 slowly. When you finish, ask the volunteers to blow out their candles, so that yours is the only one burning.

Place the candle on the chair in the center of the circle, then say: **As you've heard, there are lots of New Age beliefs about what makes you spiritual and what it means to grow spiritually. But for Christians, spirituality and spiritual growth mean something very specific and very powerful. I've invited the Spirit of Jesus here to join us today as we explore what it means for Christians to grow spiritually. He's represented by the candle on the chair. It's my**  **hope that through the experiences we'll have during this study, you'll discover that <u>true spiritual growth means becoming more like Jesus.</u>**

Lead the group in prayer, asking Jesus to join your study today and to give everyone wisdom to discern between New Age counterfeits and true spirituality.

SPIRITUAL EXPLORATION ▼

Changing Faces   (25 to 30 minutes)
Leave the large candle burning, turn on the room lights, and have kids form trios. In their trios, have each person tell

about one famous person from history he or she admires and why.

While they're talking, give each trio a roll of masking tape, paper, yarn, and an assortment of colored, nonpermanent markers. Say: **To begin our study of true spiritual growth, we're going to get some hands-on experience in becoming like someone we admire. During the next several minutes, you're going to decorate the faces of your small-group members to help each person look something like the person he or she admires.**

Have kids use the supplies creatively to make their partners resemble the person they admire. For example, if Jeff says he admires Abraham Lincoln, his partners can use the supplies to make a yarn "beard" for Jeff, then use tape to give him a bigger nose or chin.

When trios are ready, have them introduce their "celebrity make overs" to the whole group. Have kids give awards for "Best Make Over," "Most Famous-Looking," or "Most Creative Use of Tape."

As kids settle down and remove the tape from their faces, have them get their Bibles. Say: **The Bible doesn't tell us much about what Jesus looked liked, but we do know some of the key character qualities he lived by—qualities he wants us to live by as well. Psalm 1, which I read a few moments ago, shows us some qualities of true spirituality that we're going to look at more closely.**

Have trio members open their Bibles to Psalm 1 and Galatians 5:22-23. Then say: **Both of these passages reveal several inner qualities of spiritual growth. As you read these verses in your trios, look for ways these passages support the idea that <u>spiritual</u>**  **<u>growth means becoming more like Jesus.</u>**

After trios have read both passages, have them use the supplies to transform one person in their small group to "look like" Jesus, based on these passages. For example, to make someone look loving, kids can tape a heart shape on his or her chest. Or to make someone look strong, they can create big muscles and tape them onto his or her arms. Tell them they can decorate the person's whole body—carefully. When trios finish, have them discuss these questions:

● **Why did you decorate your "Jesus" person the way you did?**
● **How is this activity like "becoming like Jesus" in real life?**
● **How is it different?**
● **Most people in the New Age movement believe that through meditation or spiritual experiences, they can become like gods. Is our Christian desire to become like Jesus (who is God) the same thing? Why or why not?**
  ● **How do New Age practitioners try to become like "gods"?**
  ● **How do Christians try to become like Jesus?**
  ● **What's the difference between New Age spirituality and Christian spiritual growth?**

Say: **Real spiritual growth doesn't happen by our own efforts. But as we make our relationship with Jesus the priority in our lives, <u>he changes us to become more and more like</u>**  **<u>him.</u> That's real spiritual growth. So the question for Christians is: How do you make your relationship with Jesus a priority? Let's see if we can answer that question together.**

PERSONAL EVALUATION ▼

Jesus and Me (10 to 15 minutes) Have kids get back into the circle they formed at the beginning of the study. Place a chair in the center of the circle. Say: **Think of the best friend you've ever had—or would like to have. Imagine that person sitting in this chair. What kinds of things would you do to build trust in each other and grow closer together as friends?**

Write kids' responses on newsprint, and tape it to the wall. Some responses might include: spending time together, talking, encouraging each other, praying together, or meeting each other's needs.

Once you have five to ten specific responses, relight the "Jesus candle" and place it on the chair in the center of the circle. Turn off the lights, and say: **Now, instead of your best earthly friend, imagine again that Jesus is in this chair. Our goal is to grow spiritually by becoming more like him—and making him our best friend of all.**

Give each group member a tea-light candle, and have them light their candles from the Jesus candle. When all the candles are lit, say: **Your lighted candles represent Jesus being with you wherever you go. He is with you as a true friend and constant companion, eager to help you become more like him as you get to know him better.**

Instruct kids each to select one item from the list of ways to draw closer to a friend. As they're making their choices, distribute the "Jesus and Me" handouts (p. 22) and pencils. Then have each person move off to a place to be alone and spend a few moments getting to know Jesus better, guided by the questions on the handout.

Allow kids up to ten minutes to complete their handouts. When time is up, call everyone back to the circle. Leave the room lights off and have kids keep their candles burning, along with the Jesus candle in the center of the circle. Have volunteers tell what they discovered or experienced in this activity. After several people have shared, say: **Spiritual growth—true spirituality—means becoming more like Jesus. And as many of us have just discovered, we don't have to do it by ourselves. Jesus wants to know us and help us grow to be more like him.**

GROUP BUILDING ▼

Jesus and You (5 to 10 minutes) Have kids turn their chairs so that each person is facing a partner with the two candles burning between them.

Say: **Becoming like Jesus doesn't happen in a vacuum, because he often reveals himself through the people around us. We can grow spiritually by learning more about each other.**

Instruct the pairs to maintain silent eye-contact for one minute as they think about the Christlike character qualities they see in each other's life.

DEPTH FINDER

UNDERSTANDING THE BIBLE

One misconception young people often struggle with is that spiritual character as it's described in Galatians 5:22-23 is the result of human effort and commitment. The Apostle Paul, however, called these character qualities the "fruit of the Spirit," indicating that these inner qualities result from the Holy Spirit's working within the heart of the Christian. The fruit of the Spirit isn't something we can manufacture or do ourselves—it's the natural outgrowth of an intimate relationship with God.

When time is up, have kids maintain eye contact while they tell their partners what qualities of Jesus they see in them. For example, Joe might say to Bill, "I appreciate the love and the kindness you show people. You seem to have a genuine respect for others, just as Jesus did."

Once partners have shared, have them pray together, asking Jesus to help them both become more like him. As kids finish their prayers, encourage them to keep their candles as a reminder of Jesus' presence with them this week.

"This is because the Lord takes care of his people, but the wicked will be destroyed."
—Psalm 1:6

Jesus and Me

Set your candle in front of you as you pray this prayer:

Jesus, I want you to come and be with me now. I want to know you better, so I can become more like you. Please show me how to grow spiritually.

As you continue in an attitude of prayer, write your responses to these questions:

1. Do you believe Jesus is with you right now? Why or why not?

2. What are three things you can do to become more aware of Jesus' presence in your life?

3. If you were to let Jesus help you grow spiritually over the next month, what do you think would change about your life?

4. Does the thought of those changes excite you or frighten you? Why?

5. Do you think the passage below is true? Why or why not?

6. If you think the passage is true, what will you do about it this week?

"Happy are those who...love the Lord's teachings, and they think about those teachings day and night. They are strong, like a tree planted by a river. The tree produces fruit in season, and its leaves don't die. Everything they do will succeed."

—from Psalm 1

HOW TO BE A REAL MAN

A Creative Study— For Guys Only

■ What does it take to be a man? ■ It's a question most guys will never ask—even though they're dying to know the answer. They'll wear all the right clothes, drive the right car, keep up on all the latest sports talk, work out at the gym three times a week, and constantly strive to make enough money to impress even the most skeptical young lady. ■ But all the while, they'll still be wondering, "Do I measure up? Am I a real man? Who can tell me?" ■ This study challenges guys to examine culturally based notions of masculinity and compare them with examples of true masculinity found in the Bible. In this way, guys can discover that the true measure of a man isn't found in the strength of his body or the thickness of his wallet. ■ It's found in the purity of his heart.

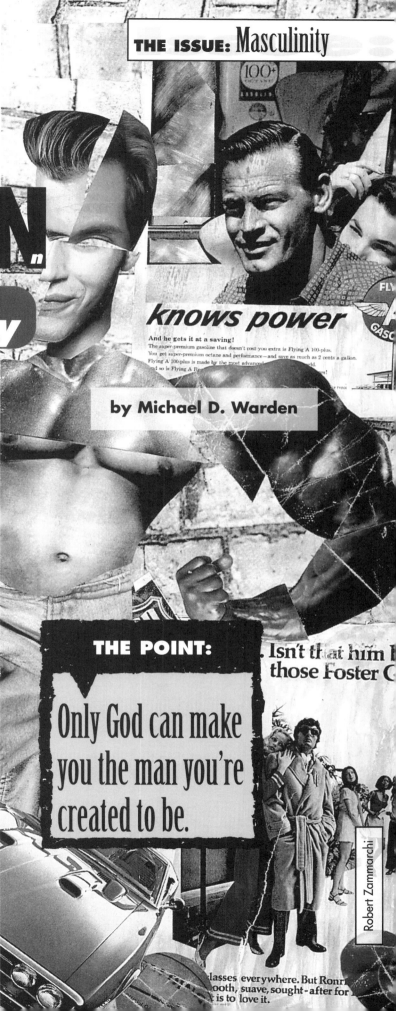

THE ISSUE: Masculinity

knows power

by **Michael D. Warden**

THE POINT:

Only God can make you the man you're created to be.

Robert Zammarchi

The Study
AT A GLANCE

SECTION	MINUTES	WHAT STUDENTS WILL DO	SUPPLIES
Relational Time	up to 5	MAN TO MAN—Share secrets about themselves no one knows.	One square-foot piece of felt for each person, markers
Creative Game	10 to 15	THE MEASURE OF A MAN—Play a game to determine whether they qualify as real men.	Masking tape, beef jerky
Bible Walk-Through	25 to 30	GIDEON, MY BROTHER—Compare their own lives with Gideon's by walking through his experience as a group.	Bibles, markers, felt squares from the first activity
Group Affirmation	10 to 15	BROTHER NAMES—Give each other new names based on positive qualities they see.	Bible, felt squares from the previous activity, markers

notes:

Only God can make you the man you're created to be.

THE BIBLE CONNECTION

| JUDGES 6–7 | God calls Gideon and makes him a mighty warrior. |
| 1 SAMUEL 16:7 | God tells Samuel how he determines the worth of a man. |

I n this study, your guys will compare the way our culture measures "manliness" with God's measure of true manhood.

By making this comparison, your young men can recognize that to be a "real man" in God's eyes, they must commit themselves to follow God and grow spiritually.

Explore the verses in The Bible Connection, then examine the information in the Depthfinder boxes throughout the study to gain a deeper understanding of how these Scriptures connect with your young people.

THE STUDY

RELATIONAL TIME ▼

Man to Man (up to 5 minutes) As guys arrive, give them each a square-foot section of felt and a marker. Have each guy write his name on his square then create a symbol that represents an embarrassing secret about himself that no one knows about. The secret could be anything from "I compulsively brush my teeth at least five times a day" to "I love watching *Scooby Doo* cartoons."

Once everyone is finished, have guys find partners and share their secrets. Then ask partners to discuss these questions:

LEADER TIP
for Man to Man

Encourage guys to keep their symbols simple. For example, a drawing of a tooth would work well for the first secret described in the text, and the letters "SD" would work for *Scooby Doo*.

● How did it feel to expose your secret?

● Why do we (as guys) sometimes have secrets about ourselves that we don't want anyone to know?

● Do you think guys generally try to project a certain image to the people around them? Why or why not?

● When guys try to project an image to the people around them, what do you think that image is like?

● Do you think guys feel pressure to have a certain attitude, have certain abilities, or behave a certain way? Why or why not?

● Do you like our culture's image of what a man should be? Why or why not?

Say: **Today we're going to explore our culture's view of masculinity and compare it with how the Bible defines a real man. Through this exploration, we're going to discover that the best way to become a real man is to commit yourself to growing spiritually, because <u>only God can make you the man you're created to be.</u>**

CREATIVE GAME ▼

LEADER TIP
for The Study

The felt squares used throughout this study can be found inexpensively at any craft store. Or, if you like, you can substitute any type of scrap cloth or even construction paper. Whatever you use, be sure to choose only light colors such as white, tan, or yellow, so kids' writing will show on them easily.

The Measure of a Man

(10 to 15 minutes)

Have guys collect their felt squares, then clear the room of all chairs and other obstacles. When the room is clear, gather everyone along one wall. Tell guys they're in the "end zone." Then ask a few volunteers to help you change the room into a playing field by laying ten parallel strips of masking tape across the floor (see diagram).

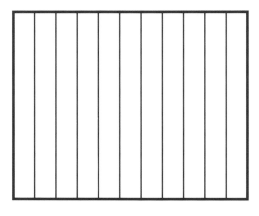

Once all the tape strips are laid, make sure all the guys are huddled in the end zone. Then say: **Before we explore what the Bible says about masculinity, let's see who can measure up to the world's standard of what it means to be a real man. I'm going to ask you a series of twelve questions. Each time you can honestly answer "yes" to a question, you can advance across one line of the playing field. If you can't answer "yes" to a question, you must remain where you are. You must answer "yes" to at least ten of these questions and make it to the other end of the room to be considered a real man. Those guys who don't make the cut don't qualify as men yet. Ready? Here we go.**

Ask the following questions one at a time. After each question, allow guys to respond by either remaining in place or moving forward. Challenge guys to be honest. Here are the questions:

1. Have you ever dunked a basketball, hit a home run, or

DEPTH FINDER
UNDERSTANDING THESE YOUNG MEN

Many speakers who talk about men's issues often refer to what is called the "wounded male soul." They say this woundedness in men stems basically from two sources:

● the absence of real relationships between fathers and sons and

● the cultural pressure men feel to be *emotionless* in order to be considered real men.

But what do these men's issues have to do with the teenage kids in your group? Everything. Your teenage guys face the same conflicting expectations that are thrust on their elders. On the one hand, they're told they need to be sensitive and compassionate, willing to hug and touch and cry whenever the situation demands it—the stereotypical '90s male.

On the other hand, your young men still feel the pressure to act tough and be assertive, competitive, and bold. Whether they're consciously aware of it or not, your guys are constantly trying to decide if they should be hard or soft, aggressive or passive, angry or loving. As Edward Gilbreath put it in Christianity Today, "Men must somehow navigate between being lions and lambs."

You can help your teenage guys find their way through the maze of public opinion about masculinity by pointing them to Jesus. He is both Lamb and Lion—the perfect example of what it means to be a man. As your young men learn to embrace and follow Christ's example of masculinity, they'll find a new freedom in their identities—to be themselves as both Christians and men.

LEADER TIP
for The Measure of a Man

This activity may cause some of your guys to feel uncomfortable. That's OK. The goal of the experience is to help guys process their anxious feelings about their masculinity. The debriefing questions at the end of the activity should help your group members process their feelings of discomfort in a positive way.

scored a touchdown?

2. Have you ever been in a fistfight?

3. Does the car you drive impress the girls at school?

4. Have you ever been a quarterback on a football team or a pitcher on a baseball team?

5. Was the last time you cried over a year ago?

6. Do girls like your massive chest and washboard stomach?

7. Do most people think you wear cool clothes?

8. Are your grades above average?

9. Have you ever been told you're a good kisser?

10. Have you ever read a book completely through, from start to finish?

11. Do you consider yourself a risk taker, especially when it comes to physical "adventure sports" such as mountain biking or rock climbing?

12. Have you ever dreamed of being a rock star or a professional athlete?

If any guys make it all the way to the other end of the room, declare them real men, and award them each a stick of beef jerky. Then have guys each find a partner near them to discuss these questions:

● **Do you think these questions were a fair test for measuring your masculinity? Why or why not?**

● **How did it feel to have your masculinity scrutinized through these questions?**

LEADER TIP
for The Measure of a Man

If you don't have time to pick up a few packets of beef jerky to award as prizes, substitute the prize by having guys award high fives to the winners.

DEPTH FINDER   UNDERSTANDING THE BIBLE

A fleece like the one Gideon used in his prayer to God is simply a "coat of wool freshly sheared from a sheep." The noun "fleece" literally means "a cutting from a lamb" or "a cutting of wool."

● **How did it feel to be compared to the other guys in the class?**

● **How is that like the way it feels to "measure your masculinity" against other guys in real life?**

● **Do you think you know what it takes to be a real man? Explain.**

● **How would you define true masculinity?**

● **How do you think God would define true masculinity?**

● **What would it take for you to become a real man in God's eyes?**

After partners discuss the final question, say: **In a moment, we're going to take a look at the life of one young man in the Bible who didn't think very highly of himself as a man. But God saw a potential in him that no one else did and called him to change the history of an entire nation. His name was Gideon, and because he was willing to follow God, Gideon discovered that God was the only one who had the power to make him into the man he was created to be.**

BIBLE WALK-THROUGH ▼

Gideon, My Brother (25 to 30 minutes) Gather guys back to the "end zone" where they started the previous game. Give everyone a Bible and a marker, and have guys get their felt squares from the first activity. Tell guys you're going to have another kind of race, only this time they'll be racing to sculpt certain shapes out of their felt squares.

Have guys set their Bibles on the floor in front of them. Then say: **Here's how the race works. I'll call out an item for you to sculpt using only your felt square. The first guy to create a believable representation of the item I call out will read a passage from Gideon's story (which is found in Judges 6 and 7). After reading the passage, I'll ask a question or two. Then we'll all step over the first line of the playing field and do the process again—this time creating a different object and reading a different passage about Gideon. We'll continue until we reach the other end of the room.**

Once guys understand, start the activity by following these instructions:

1. While in the end zone, have guys race to create an angel with their felt squares. Have the winner of the race read aloud Judges 6:11-16. Then have guys find partners and discuss these questions:

● **How did Gideon react to being called a mighty warrior by God?**

● **How would you react if God called you a mighty warrior?**

2. Have guys cross the first line of the playing field then race to sculpt a goat using their felt squares. Have the winner read aloud Judges 6:17-19. Then have guys each turn to a partner and discuss this question:

● **If you heard God say that you had the heart of a great warrior, what kind of proof would you need before you'd believe God had really spoken to you?**

3. Have guys cross the next line of the playing field then race to sculpt a rock using their felt squares. Have the winner read aloud Judges 6:20-24. Then have guys find partners and discuss this question:

● **Why do you think the angel chose to "dazzle" Gideon in this way?**

4. Have guys cross the next line of the playing field then race to sculpt a pole using their felt squares. Have the winner read aloud Judges 6:25-28. Then have guys form pairs and discuss these questions:

● **Gideon acted like a coward by waiting until dark to do what the angel instructed. Have you ever felt like a coward? Explain.**

● **Since God knew that Gideon would act this way, why did the angel call him a mighty warrior?**

5. Have guys cross the next line of the playing field then race to sculpt a trumpet using their felt squares. Have the winner read aloud Judges 6:33-35. Then have guys each turn to a partner and discuss these questions:

● **Gideon became very brave once the Holy Spirit "entered" Gideon. What does that tell you about the connection between spiritual growth and true masculinity?**

● **If <u>only God can make you the man you're created to be,</u> what should your relationship with him be like?**

6. Have guys cross the next line of the playing field then hold out their felt squares in front of them. While guys look at their squares, read aloud Judges 6:36-40. Then say: **<u>God wants to make you into the man he created you to be,</u> but he can't do that unless you learn to trust him. In this passage, Gideon used a fleece to help him learn to trust God. What will it take for you to <u>trust God to make you the man he wants you to be?</u> On your felt "fleece," write a short prayer that describes what you'd like God to do to help you believe in him more. When you're finished, share your prayer with a partner.**

7. Have guys cross the next line of the playing field then race to sculpt a cup using their felt squares. Have the winner read aloud Judges 7:1-7. Then have guys each turn to a partner and discuss this question:

● **Would you have been willing to obey God the way Gideon did in this passage? Why or why not?**

8. Have guys cross the next line of the playing field then race to sculpt a tent using their felt squares. Have the winner read aloud Judges 7:8-15. Then have guys form pairs and discuss this question:

● **Based on this passage, how do you think God wants men to deal with their fears?**

9. Have guys cross the next line of the playing field then race to sculpt a sword using their felt squares. Have the winner read aloud Judges 7:16-25. Then have guys find partners and discuss these questions:

LEADER TIP

for Gideon, My Brother

As you go through Gideon's story, avoid choosing the same few guys each time as the sculpture winners. Instead, spread the victory around to several people in the class. That way, more of your group members will get to read the Scriptures and participate more directly in the activity.

- **Based on this passage, would you say Gideon was a real man? Why or why not?**
- **What caused Gideon to change from the scared young farmer into the mighty warrior he became?**
- **What would cause you to change to become the man God created you to be?**

Have guys cross the next line of the playing field, then say: **Gideon's example shows us that <u>only God can make you the man he created you to be.</u> As we follow his commands and commit to growing in our relationship with him, we'll be changed into real men—just like Gideon was.**

GROUP AFFIRMATION ▼

Brother Names

(10 to 15 minutes)
Form groups of four or fewer, and have groups move to different parts of the room. Read aloud 1 Samuel 16:7, then say: **God doesn't measure masculinity the way our culture does. He doesn't care about the style of your clothes or the size of your biceps. He cares about the character of your heart. When the angel appeared to Gideon, Gideon looked scared and weak on the outside, but God looked into his heart and saw a mighty warrior. Let's close today by giving each other brand new names—like mighty warrior—based on the positive qualities we see in each other's hearts.**

Have each group pick one other group of guys in the room to rename. (Make sure no group is left out.) Have group members work together to come up with a new name for each person in their assigned group, based on that person's best inner qualities. For example, a group might give someone the name Kind Encourager, Bold Speaker, or Seeker of God. Once each group has come up with the names, have those group members go to their assigned group and write each new name on the appropriate person's felt square.

Encourage guys to keep their felt square "fleeces" tacked to the wall above their beds, as a constant reminder to seek God, so they can grow to become the men God created them to be.

TrueBeauty

Helping Girls Learn How to Become Women

by Amy Simpson

A Creative Study– For Girls Only

THE POINT:

> Only God can make you the woman you're created to be.

■ It's a confusing world. Today's teenage girls are hearing so many messages about what it means to be a woman: beauty, sex, power, motherhood, money, love, a perfect body, marriage, subservience, the latest fashions. In a world scarred by the battle of the sexes, it seems everyone has an agenda when it comes to helping girls grow up. In a society where we are all so strongly influenced by the media, politics, and the power of image, growing up has become more than a matter of "like mother, like daughter." For many young women, in fact, following in their mothers' footsteps is their greatest fear. Who can they look to so they can understand what it means to be the women God created them to be? ■ Today's teenage girls need to know that God has created each of them as an individual masterpiece. Girls also need to learn that only God can make them the women they were created to be. Growing in their relationships with God and learning to recognize God's presence in the lives of others can help them become Christlike women. ■ This study provides an opportunity for teenage girls to study God's Word, examine the messages they hear from others about who they should be, and look at what God says about the kind of women they should strive to be. As a result, they will be encouraged to respond to this knowledge by looking to God for their identity and looking to Christlike people for examples.

The Study
AT A GLANCE

SECTION	MINUTES	WHAT STUDENTS WILL DO	SUPPLIES
Opener	7 to 10	WHO DO YOU SAY I AM?—Create "diagrams" representing various characteristics that other people think they should have.	Markers, newsprint
Bible Study	12 to 15	THE MODEL—Study Proverbs 31:10-31 and list characteristics of "the ideal woman," then restate them in modern terms.	Bibles, pencils, paper, newsprint, tape, marker
	12 to 15	FASHION SHOW—Create and model "costumes" that demonstrate characteristics God wants them to have.	Bibles, toilet paper, string, aluminum foil, marker, newsprint list from "The Model" activity
	5 to 10	MAKEOVER—Use characteristics found in Bible study to make new "diagrams" and compare them to the diagrams created in the "Who Do You Say I Am?" activity.	Outline from "Who Do You Say I Am?" activity, markers
Personal Application	5 to 10	TUNING THEM OUT—Select objects that represent messages they've been hearing, then suggest ways for each other to overcome those messages.	Various symbolic objects
Closing	up to 5	SHOW ME THE WAY—Think of mentors or examples they can follow.	Paper, pencils

notes:

Only God can make you the woman you're created to be.

THE BIBLE CONNECTION

PROVERBS 27:1-6	This passage describes wise behavior.
PROVERBS 31:10-31	This passage describes a woman of noble character.
GALATIANS 5:22-26	This passage lists the "fruits of the Spirit."
COLOSSIANS 3:12-17	This passage lists characteristics God's people should have.

I n this study, girls will examine some of the messages they hear about what it means to be a woman. They'll look at what God says about who they should be, compare this to the messages they often hear, and determine how to begin listening to God's voice instead of the expectations of others.

By learning what God says about noble character, girls can understand that only God can make them the women they were created to be and learn to pursue God's plans for their lives.

Explore the verses in The Bible Connection, then examine the information in the Depthfinder boxes throughout the study to gain a deeper understanding of how these Scriptures connect with your young people.

BEFORE THE STUDY

Before the study, gather a collection of objects that represent various messages girls hear about what makes a real woman; for example, you may include objects such as an apron, a briefcase, mascara, a soccer ball, a baby bottle, a dollar bill, a wedding veil, and birth control.

LEADER TIP for The Study

Because this topic can be so powerful and relevant to kids' lives, your group members may be tempted to get caught up in issues and lose sight of the deeper biblical principle found in The Point. Help your kids grasp The Point by guiding kids to focus on the biblical investigation and discussing how God's truth connects with reality in their lives.

THE STUDY

OPENER ▼

Who Do You Say I Am? (7 to 10 minutes)

Have girls form five groups. Give each group markers and a large sheet of newsprint. Have each group trace around one person on its newsprint. Then assign each group one of the following influences: mom, dad, television and movies, teachers, and guys.

Instruct each group to label its newsprint person according to the characteristics they think their assigned people want them to have. For example, the "television and movies" group might write "thin body" next to the hips or waist, "perfect teeth" next to the mouth, and "beautiful hair" next to the head.

When everyone is finished, have each group present its diagram to the other groups, pointing out and explaining the characteristics they described. Encourage groups to clap for each other's presentations.

When groups are finished making their presentations, ask:

● **What sources pressure you to be a certain type of person or to meet specific standards?**

● **What kinds of messages do you hear about what makes a real woman?**

● **What are some positive expectations for women?**

● **What are some negative expectations?**

● **How much do you think other people can tell you about what kind of person you should be?**

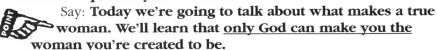

Say: **Today we're going to talk about what makes a true woman. We'll learn that <u>only God can make you the woman you're created to be.</u>**

BIBLE STUDY ▼

The Model (12 to 15 minutes)

Have girls form pairs. Divide the twenty-two verses of Proverbs 31:10-31 among the pairs. Give each pair a pencil and paper.

Say: **With your partner, read aloud the verses I've assigned you. Then look in those verses for characteristics that describe what "the ideal woman" should be like. List those characteristics on a piece of paper. You'll have a minute to compile your list.**

As kids work, tape two sheets of newsprint to the wall. After a minute, have each group read its list aloud and explain the meaning of its assigned verses. As each group reads its list, write the characteristics on one of the sheets of newsprint.

Then say: **Now let's talk about what each of these characteristics**

As teenagers, girls experience a crucial stage in the development of their self-concept. As they begin to experience life in the transition to adulthood, they develop much of what becomes their lifelong sense of identity.

According to Dr. Carol J. Eagle and Carol Colman in *All That She Can Be*, this identity-formation is at an especially crucial time when girls are between the ages of fourteen and sixteen: "The middle adolescent girl is opening herself up to a world of possibilities. She daydreams a lot about the kind of woman she wants to become. As she looks for a positive identity, the teenage girl flirts with many different potential careers and lifestyles.

"An after-school job in a hospital may trigger an interest in medicine or nursing; a sales job in a dress shop may steer her toward retailing; a successful experience as a counselor in a summer camp may lead her to consider teaching. A normal girl of this age is going to fantasize about many different options, and although some parents may view this as being 'flighty,' it is an important step in her quest for identity. Only by being allowed to try on different roles will she eventually find the ones with which she is comfortable."

If you are a woman, be aware that the girls you minister to are watching you carefully as a potential example for them. Your relationships with them can give them a flesh-and-blood definition of what it means to be a Christlike woman.

means in today's terms. For example, a characteristic like "She makes linen clothes and sells them" may be translated to mean "She uses her talents to provide for herself, her family, and others."

Address each characteristic on your list, encouraging girls to think of ways that characteristic can apply to them in their everyday lives. As girls come up with "translations," list them on the other sheet of newsprint.

Say: **You've come up with some excellent examples of what a Christian woman is like. Proverbs 31:10-31 offers some excellent guidelines. It's exciting to see that <u>God can make you the woman you're created to be.</u>**

Fashion Show (12 to 15 minutes)

Have girls form three new groups. Assign each group one of the following Scripture passages: Proverbs 27:1-6; Galatians 5:22-26; and Colossians 3:12-17. Give each group a Bible, a roll of toilet paper, a piece of string, and aluminum foil.

Say: **In your group, read aloud the Scripture passage I've assigned to you. Then pick one person in your group and "clothe" her in a costume (of toilet paper, string, and foil) that represents the characteristics described in your Scripture passage. In a few minutes, we'll have a fashion show, so be creative. You'll have ten minutes to complete your outfit.**

As girls work on their costumes, encourage groups to illustrate practical applications of the characteristics. For example, they may illustrate

DEPTH FINDER — UNDERSTANDING THESE GIRLS

While relationships between teenage girls and female youth workers are crucial, equally important are the relationships these girls have with male youth workers. A healthy relationship with adults of the opposite sex can help set a pattern for the rest of a teenager's life.

In *Breaking the Gender Barrier in Youth Ministry*, Jim Burns points out, "Healthy, positive youth work is most often based on positive, healthy role models. Not to oversimplify, but almost all long-lasting results in youth ministry are based not so much on programs as on relationships.

"Why it has taken some churches so long to figure out that students need healthy, positive role models from both genders is a mystery. Unfortunately, until recent years, youth ministry was mainly a "male thing." Without providing both female and male leadership, we've done a disservice to the church and our students. Same sex role models are absolutely essential for good youth ministry and good role modeling of the Christian life. At the same time, because so much youth work is modeling, we also need healthy opposite sex role models. In today's world, where can a young woman or young man build a relationship with someone of the opposite sex in a safe, secure, healthy, Christ-centered atmosphere?"

If you're a man in youth ministry, realize that you have a significant role in the lives of the girls you minister to. While it is always wise to maintain a healthy balance and to follow precautions in developing relationships with teenage girls, the life you model for them will help them understand what it means to live as the women God created them to be.

gentleness by wrapping a girl's hands with toilet paper to indicate a soft touch.

After ten minutes, have groups present a "fashion show," displaying their characteristic costumes for each other. As they list characteristics, add them to the newsprint list from the previous activity. When each group has modeled its costume, lead the other groups in a round of applause. Ask:

● **Models, how did it feel to parade your outfits for the other groups?**

● **How did the rest of you feel as you watched your creations being modeled?**

● **How do you think God feels when we display his goodness in our everyday lives?**

● **How do others feel when we show them the women God created us to be?**

● **What characteristics would you like others to notice in you?**

Say: **Now that we know that only God can make you the woman you're created to be, let's take a closer look at how you can become that woman.**

Makeover (5 to 10 minutes)

Retrieve one of the outlines the girls created in the "Who Do You Say I Am?" activity. Set the outline face down on the floor. Ask a volunteer to lie on the blank side of the newsprint while you trace an outline of her body. Give each person a marker. Point out the list of characteristics you've compiled throughout the study. Assign each characteristic to a girl until you run out of characteristics.

When each characteristic has been assigned, say: **Using the characteristic or characteristics assigned you, let's create another "diagram" on this outline. Use your characteristics to label the appropriate body parts. When we're finished, we should have a fairly complete diagram of the kind of person God wants each one of us to be.**

If girls need help applying their characteristics to specific body parts, give them practical guidance. When the diagram is complete, ask:

● **How does this diagram compare to the diagrams we created in the first activity?**

● **What kind of person does God want each one of us to be?**

● **How can we learn to apply these general characteristics to specific situations in our lives?**

● **How do you think each person's individual personality affects God's plan for the kind of woman she should be?**

● **How can you become the kind of woman God created you to be?**

Say: **Only God can make you the woman you're created**  **to be.** As you get to know God better and learn to listen to his voice rather than the messages of people around you, you'll become more like the woman he wants you to be.

PERSONAL APPLICATION ▼

Tuning Them Out (5 to 10 minutes)

Have girls form a circle. In the middle of the circle, place a collection of objects that represent various messages girls hear about what makes a real woman. For example, you may include objects such as an apron, a briefcase, mascara, a soccer ball, a baby bottle, a dollar bill, a wedding veil, and birth control.

Say: **I'd like each one of you to take a turn picking an object that represents a negative message you've received about what you should be. As you hold your object, the rest of us will suggest ways you can learn to overcome and tune out that message. As we do so, let's remind each other that only God can make us the women we're created to be. I'll start.**

Pick an object from the pile in the middle of the circle, and hold it up so everyone can see it. Ask for suggestions of ways you might overcome the messages you're hearing about what makes you a real woman. Encourage the girl next to you to pick an object, then continue the process for the rest of the group.

LEADER TIP
for Tuning Them Out

During this activity, encourage girls to be open and honest. The best way to do this is to set a real example of honesty yourself. Be open about a message you hear about what it means to be a woman. After you do so, be prepared for what may be shocking revelations from the teenage girls. As they share, be sure to respond with compassion and respect rather than shock or disgust.

DEPTH FINDER — UNDERSTANDING THE BIBLE

Proverbs 31:10-31 is often referred to as a description of "the perfect woman." In reading this passage, many assume the writer is describing a quiet, subservient, one-dimensional woman. Closer study, though, reveals a different kind of woman.

In *The 365-Day Devotional Commentary*, Lawrence O. Richards says of this woman, "While the primary focus of her activities was the family needs, this Old Testament wife is also an entrepreneur.

"The passage also makes it clear that the wife is free to make use of the profits from her enterprise. The wife's complete control of her earnings is illustrated by her generosity....In modern terms, she's set up a charitable foundation to distribute some of her profits to those less fortunate.

"What is so striking about the Proverbs 31 description is that it so powerfully contradicts the view of some Christians that a good wife must stay home, have babies, and keep busy with housework. Proverbs 31 shows us a woman of the Old Testament who is in fact a businesswoman, using her talents and abilities to the fullest, and performing the same kind of tasks that the men of that society performed."

LEADER TIP

for Show Me the Way

You may want to compile a list beforehand of people in your church or community who are willing to be mentors for the girls in your group. You can give them an opportunity during this activity to look at the list and choose mentors they would like to connect with. Your follow-up could start a meaningful and fruitful mentoring ministry in your church.

CLOSING ▼

Show Me the Way (up to 5 minutes)

Have girls remain in a circle. Say: **As we close, I want to encourage each one of you to find a mentor or an example you can follow. It's a good idea to ask a woman you know if she will be your mentor, helping you become the woman God created you to be. If you don't know anyone who is willing to be a good mentor for you, think of someone—alive or dead—who can be an example for you to follow. It's a good idea to choose a mentor or example who has interests and accomplishments similar to the ones you want to pursue.**

Give each girl a piece of paper and a pencil. Say: **Find a partner, and think with your partner about who you might follow as a mentor or an example. When you've thought of a woman, write down her name on your piece of paper.**

After a few minutes, say: **Now spend some time talking with your partner about how you can allow <u>God to make you and your partner the women God created you to be.</u> When you're finished talking, pray with your partner, asking God to make you the women you were created to be.**

Even

Super Heroes

Need Sidekicks

Understanding Our Need for One Another

by Siv M. Ricketts

THE POINT:

You need others to help you grow spiritually.

■ Ask teenagers around the world what the three most important things in their lives are, and friends will almost always be on their lists. Of course, friendship is important to people of all ages. We all need to know that we are accepted and loved by others. But your teenagers' friends have an incredible amount of influence over them—over the way they think, the way they talk, and the things they do. Their parents worry about the kinds of negative influences they find in friends. But their friends can also be a positive influence. ■ That's where accountability comes in. Christian kids need to realize that they're not alone in their venture with God. They need friends who are striving to grow in faith and will encourage them along the way. It's through accountability that students can see a reflection of what Christ wants them to be. This study will show students that in accountable relationships, they can feel God's love reaching to them and changing them.

The Study
AT A GLANCE

SECTION	MINUTES	WHAT STUDENTS WILL DO	SUPPLIES
Opening Experience	10 to 15	TWO ARE STRONGER THAN ONE—Demonstrate how much stronger they are together than individually.	
Bible Experience	20 to 25	WEAVING TRUE FRIENDSHIP—Discover characteristics that are important in Christian relationships, and create a braid that demonstrates weaving these characteristics into one.	Bibles, "What Makes a Good Friend?" handout strips (pp. 46-47), pencils, yarn or string, tape
	5 to 10	WALKING THE LINE—See how far they can walk on their hands and how much farther they can go with the help of a friend.	Snacks, braids created in "Weaving True Friendship" activity
Closing Experience	5 to 10	ACCOUNTABILITY COMMITMENTS—Prepare an agreement to give to a person who will hold them accountable.	Pencils, paper, "Accountability Agreement" handouts (p. 48)

notes:

You need others to help you grow spiritually.

THE BIBLE CONNECTION

ECCLESIASTES 4:9-12	This passage lists some of the reasons we need each other.
PROVERBS 13:20; 24:26; 27:17; MATTHEW 18:15; JOHN 15:12-13; 1 CORINTHIANS 12:14-20, 27; 13:4-8; EPHESIANS 4:15; PHILIPPIANS 2:2-5; HEBREWS 10:24-25	These passages describe attributes that are important in relationships.

I n this study, kids will demonstrate how much stronger two are than one, braid together characteristics that make a strong Christian relationship, and evaluate their friendships and lives to determine who should hold them accountable.

By doing this, kids can understand the importance of having another growing Christian walk alongside them as they live Christian lives.

Explore the verses in The Bible Connection, then examine the information in the Depthfinder boxes throughout the study to gain a deeper understanding of how these Scriptures connect with your young people.

BEFORE THE STUDY

Make one photocopy for each student of the "What Makes a Good Friend?" handout (pp. 46-47), and cut the handouts into eight strips. Paper clip similar strips together so the sections don't get mixed up. Also cut enough two-foot lengths of yarn or string so each group of four can have three pieces.

LEADER TIP for The Study

Because this topic can be so powerful and relevant to kids' lives, your group members may be tempted to get caught up in issues and lose sight of the deeper biblical principle found in The Point. Help your kids grasp The Point by guiding kids to focus on the biblical investigation and discussing how God's truth connects with reality in their lives.

THE STUDY

LEADER TIP

for The Study

Whenever groups discuss a list of questions, write the questions on newsprint and tape the newsprint to the wall so groups can discuss the questions at their own pace.

LEADER TIP

for Weaving True Friendship

If you have more than twenty-four kids in your group, consider sub-dividing the four groups. Have kids work on the same "What Makes a Good Friend?" handout strips, but have kids discuss the answers with no more than six kids per group. If you have less than eight students, have kids work on the handout strips individually as needed.

OPENING EXPERIENCE ▼

Two Are Stronger Than One (10 to 15 minutes)

Ask students to pair up with someone of the same gender. Say: **Have one person in your pair sit on the floor and make his or her body as small and tight as possible without holding on to anything. If you're sitting on the floor, your goal is to prevent your partner from pushing you outside an imaginary circle that immediately surrounds you. You can't use your arms to prevent your partner from pushing you out of the circle. The person doing the pushing must be gentle and must move his or her partner with the utmost care.** Allow students to push their partners out of the "circles." Reverse roles and repeat the activity.

Have partners pair up with other pairs of the same gender to form groups of four. Say: **We'll do the activity again, but this time both you and your partner will sit inside the circle. You can hold on to each other and the other pair will try to gently push you both out of the circle.** Repeat the activity so that both pairs take turns pushing and being pushed.

Have the groups discuss the following questions:

● **Was it easy or difficult to push your partner out of his or her imaginary circle? Why?**

● **How was it different when there were two people to push out of the circle? Explain.**

● **How did the activity represent the importance of relationships?**

● **How important is it to have Christian friends? Explain.**

● **How can having a Christian friend stick by you help you grow spiritually?**

Say: **We are stronger when we have others to help us. And we need others to help us grow spiritually.** Today we're going to learn more about accountability—being responsible to a friend for our actions—and what that looks like in our friendships. Before we move on, tell the person on your left how you've seen him or her stick with friends, or why you think he or she would be a good friend to stick with.

DEPTHFINDER MUTUAL ACCOUNTABILITY

To have friends, you have to be a friend. Remind your students that the kind of characteristics they look for in an accountability partner should also be characteristics that they're pursuing (or willing to pursue) in their own lives. They can't be the kind of friend who measures up to God's standards unless they are actively involved in a relationship with God.

If you don't already know how to braid three strands, you'll want to practice before class. Have someone hold the knotted end of three strands or tape it to a table. Begin by placing the right strand over the middle strand, so that it becomes the new middle strand. Then place the left strand over the middle strand, so that it becomes the middle strand. Alternate placing right over middle and left over middle until your braid is the desired length. Knot the end of the braid to keep it from unraveling.

BIBLE EXPERIENCE ▼

Weaving True Friendship (20 to 25 minutes)

Have the students from each group of four go to four different areas in your room. Assign a number from one to four to each area. While teens are moving, pass out pencils to all the students. Then distribute the "What Makes a Good Friend?" handout strips (pp. 46-47) to the corresponding areas so that each student has two strips.

Say: **With your new group, read the passages listed on your strips and answer the questions. You should make notes on your strips because you'll use the information later.**

Give kids about eight minutes to answer the questions before instructing them to return to their original foursomes. Give each group three two-foot lengths of yarn or string and some tape. Tell students to match up the ends of their pieces of yarn and tie a knot at one end to hold all three together.

Say: **While one of you holds the knot, have another group member begin a braid. Then take turns securing one strip of paper at a time to the middle strand. Fold the blank edge of the strip around the yarn and tape it to the back so that all the words can still be seen, and then continue braiding. As you attach each strip to the braid, share with your group what you learned.**

When the braids are done, have students read Ecclesiastes 4:9-12 and discuss the following questions:
● **What are some benefits of having close Christian friends?**
● **According to these verses, why do <u>you need others to</u> <u>grow spiritually?</u>**
● **How does your braid represent Ecclesiastes 4:12?**

Say: **Building relationships in which you're comfortable sharing your weaknesses takes time and effort, just as it took some concentration and effort to create your braids. But it pays off when you find that you have a friend you can trust walking with you through the tough times. Let me show you what I mean.**

Walking the Line (5 to 10 minutes)

Ask students to join their braids end to end in a line on the floor. Have students form a line at one end of the braids. Set a snack at the opposite end.

COMPLETED BRAID

LEADER TIP
for Walking the Line

If you have fewer than sixteen students, have kids leave six to twelve inches between the ends of each braid as they lay them on the floor.

Say: **All you have to do to get this snack is to walk along these braids to the end of the line. Each of you will have an opportunity to walk along the braids. There is, of course, a catch. You must walk on your hands as you go down the line. Do I have any volunteers?** Allow volunteers to walk on their hands down the line. Replace the snack each time a volunteer reaches the end. After all of the volunteers have had a chance to go, tell students to get with a partner and walk the line "wheelbarrow" style (one student walks on his or her hands while the student behind holds his or her feet up). Have partners switch roles and walk the line again. Give a snack to all the students.

When all pairs have had a turn, discuss these questions:

● **What kinds of things are easier to do alone? with the help of others?**

● **How is this activity like how Christians can stick together and encourage each other?**

● **How is it different?**

● **What do you think it means to hold someone accountable?** Call kids back together. Ask:

● **What does a healthy relationship that includes two Christian friends and Jesus look like?**

Say: **For most of you, it was much easier to walk the line when you had help. The Christian walk is the same way. Relationships of accountability help us to keep walking when we're tired. They help bring balance to our lives by showing us our mistakes. They give us a sense of safety and security when we feel help-less or alone. We need others to help us grow spiritually.**

LEADER TIP
for Walking the Line

You may want to provide a belt or a piece of rope for students to use to prevent their shirts from falling down as they walk on their hands. Or you can remind students to tuck their shirts in before they begin.

CLOSING EXPERIENCE ▼

Accountability Commitments (5 to 10 minutes)

Say: **We all need others to keep us accountable in what we do and who we become. Let's do an exercise that will help all of us find others who will keep us accountable in our walks with God.**

Give each student a pencil, a sheet of paper, and a copy of the "Accountability Agreement" handout (p. 48). Ask kids to spread out as much as the room allows.

When students are seated again say: **On your paper, list three close friends or people you admire of any age.** Pause for a moment to allow students to reflect.

Say: **Now ask yourself whether the people on your list have characteristics that line up with the characteristics written on the braids we created. Remember, no one is perfect, but it's important to look for friends who at least try to measure up to God's standards. In order for someone to help you grow spiritually, they have to be growing also.**

After a minute, say: **Evaluate your life and areas in which you need help. You might include positive behaviors that you want to**

LEADER TIP
for Walking the Line

To protect students from injury, consider asking two students to act as spotters as kids attempt to walk down the line. Instruct the spotters to intervene only when the person walking down the line is about to fall in a way that may cause injury.

DEPTHFINDER — FORGIVENESS

Peter was one of Jesus' best friends. He and his brother were the first disciples Jesus called. He walked with Jesus on the water. He was present at the transfiguration and in the garden of Gethsemane when Jesus was arrested. Peter swore to Jesus that his faith would never waver. But before Jesus' death, Peter denied three times that he even knew Jesus. Peter blew it as a friend. Even so, after Jesus rose from the dead, he forgave Peter and gave him the mandate to care for God's people.

Ephesians 4:32 says, "Be kind and loving to each other, and forgive each other just as God forgave you in Christ." Just as Jesus forgave Peter, he's also forgiven us, and so we need to forgive our friends when they don't measure up to the standards set for relationships of accountability. We must remember how much God has forgiven us and follow his example.

LEADER TIP for Walking the Line

It's OK if no one volunteers to walk the line on his or her own. Wait for about a minute before having kids go down the line with partners. Use the discomfort the kids may feel from your request to talk about the discomfort, fear, and difficulties that come from doing things without the help or support of others.

keep, like daily devotions or attending church, or bad habits that you want to quit. You can also evaluate your life against the characteristics you wrote on the braids you created and see where you need improvement. When you've got at least three areas in which you need help, complete the Accountability Agreement card, addressing it to one of the people that closely matched the braid characteristics.

Instruct the students to ask the people they've chosen to keep them accountable to sign the agreements. Encourage kids to tell the people who sign the agreements why <u>we need others to help us grow spiritually</u>. Challenge kids to have their agreements completed by your next meeting.

DEPTHFINDER — ACCOUNTABILITY AND DATING

Ecclesiastes 4:12 is often quoted in marriage ceremonies as a man and woman enter into a relationship before God. As a husband and wife learn to love and submit to each other and to God, their relationship should be one of accountability. Remind teens that the standards for friendship also apply to marriage relationships and dating relationships.

LEADER TIP for Walking the Line

When the lesson is over, you can use the braids to decorate your meeting room as a reminder of the importance of having friends who help us to grow spiritually.

What Makes a  Friend?

Area One: 1 Corinthians 13:4-8

● Do you and your friends love each other? If so, how do you show love for each other?
● Choose one of the attributes of Christlike love from 1 Corinthians 13, and discuss ideas about how you can become more loving in that way.

Area One: John 15:12-13

● What are three ways Jesus has shown his love for you?
● What difference would it make to your relationships if you loved as Jesus loves?
● On the back of this strip, list at least three ways you can help your friends grow spiritually.

Area Two: Proverbs 24:26; Matthew 18:15

● What are the benefits of honesty in relationships? the consequences of dishonesty?
  Share a personal example.
● Is it easy or difficult to be honest with your friends? Explain.

Area Two: Ephesians 4:15

● Give an example of how you could speak the truth in love to a friend who...
  ● has stopped attending church.
  ● talked badly about you behind your back.
  ● is involved in a hurtful dating relationship.
● What's the difference between speaking the truth in love and controlling your friends?
● On the back of this strip, list at least three ways you can help your friends grow spiritually.

Area Three: 1 Corinthians 12:14-20, 27

● How does it affect your picture of your friendships (your youth group, your church) to think of them as a physical body?
● What part of the body does the person on your right occupy in their friendships? For example, if they're a good listener, they could be an ear.

Area Three: Philippians 2:2-5

● What can you do to have one mind and purpose with your friends?
● How would humbling yourself and giving more honor to others affect your relationships?
● On the back of this strip, list at least three ways you can help your friends grow spiritually.

Area Four: Proverbs 13:20; 27:17

● How can your friendships make you a better person? How might they get you in trouble?
● How can you know if your friends are wise?

Area Four: Hebrews 10:24-25

● Why is it important to have friends at church?
● Brainstorm at least four good deeds you can do to show love to your friends.
● On the back of this strip, list at least three ways you can help your friends grow spiritually.

What Makes a Good Friend?

ACCOUNTABILITY AGREEMENT

DATE:_____

I would like _____ to hold me accountable to the following three things:

- _____

- _____

- _____

Signed: _____

I agree to hold _____ accountable for the above three things.

Signed: _____

Remember Who You Are

Helping Kids Understand Their Identity as God's Children

■ In his book *All Grown Up & No Place to Go*, David Elkind laments, "Teenagers now are expected to confront life and its challenges with the maturity once expected only of the middle-aged." He's right. Did *you* spend your high school years worrying about AIDS? Did you have to walk through a metal detector before you went to class? Did you ever

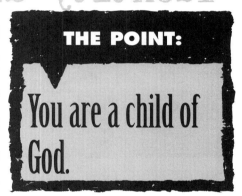

THE POINT:

You are a child of God.

consider downloading pornography from the Internet while you were at school? ■ Most of your kids have already made decisions regarding sex, alcohol, and drugs. They're growing up too fast. The strain and stress of a lost childhood has produced teenagers who are tired and desperate for a place of rest—a place of safety where they can believe, trust, and just be kids. ■ Fortunately, God has called them to such a place. Through the sacrifice of Jesus Christ, God has provided your kids with the opportunity to hope again. Your teenagers can rest in childlike faith of God's complete love, faithfulness, and care. This study will help your kids walk in the knowledge that they are children of God and the assurance that they can come to the Father like innocent and optimistic children. It will help your kids realize that much of their spiritual growth comes through having faith like a child.

by Bill and Brooke Fisher

The Study
AT A GLANCE

SECTION	MINUTES	WHAT STUDENTS WILL DO	SUPPLIES
Opening Experience	5 to 10	LET'S PLAY!—Play a child's game similar to Duck, Duck, Goose, and discuss what it means to be childlike.	Bible
Bible Experiences	5 to 10	GOD THE F·A·T·H·E·R—Compare earthly fathers to God.	Bibles, pencils, paper, newsprint, tape, marker
	20 to 25	NO NEWS IS GOOD NEWS—compare newspaper facts and headlines to relevant statistics and applicable Scriptures.	Bibles, pencils, paper, newspapers, newsprint, tape, marker, "Do I Have to Grow Up?" handouts (p. 56)
Reflection	10 to 15	THE JOURNEY—Follow the path of balloons to get to the other side of the room, discuss their accessibility to God, and pray.	Bible, balloons, markers, paper, tape

notes:

You are a child of God.

THE BIBLE CONNECTION

PSALM 68:4-6; ISAIAH 45:18-19; MATTHEW 7:9-11; EPHESIANS 2:4-7	These verses describe God.
MALACHI 4:2, 5-6; JOHN 10:9-10; 1 CORINTHIANS 6:18-20; EPHESIANS 4:22-24	These passages offer hope to Christians.
MARK 10:13-15	These verses explain that we must become like children.
ROMANS 8:15-17	These verses explain that we are God's children.
HEBREWS 10:19-23	These verses explain that we can come near to God because of Jesus' death.

I n this study, students will play a child's game, compare earthly fathers to God, look at the messages they receive about the world, and take a "journey" to get to God.

Through these experiences, your kids can discover that they are children of God and that they can hope, trust, and communicate with God because of their irrevocable identity as his children.

Explore the verses in The Bible Connection, then examine the information in the Depthfinder boxes throughout the study to gain a deeper understanding of how these Scriptures connect with your young people.

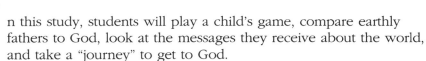

THE STUDY

OPENING EXPERIENCE ▼

Let's Play! (5 to 10 minutes)
Have teenagers form a circle and sit down. Say: **We're going to start with a game that's a lot like Duck, Duck, Goose. But**

LEADER TIP for The Study

Because this topic can be so powerful and relevant to kids' lives, your group members may be tempted to get caught up in issues and lose sight of the deeper biblical principle found in The Point. Help your kids grasp The Point by guiding kids to focus on the biblical investigation and discussing how God's truth connects with reality in their lives.

instead of saying, "duck, duck, goose," the person who is "It" will say words that describe something he or she really enjoyed as a child. For example, let's say the person who is It enjoyed swimming and dolls. It will walk around the circle, tapping the shoulders of each person in the circle. Each time It taps a shoulder, he or she will say "swimming." When It taps someone on the shoulder and says "dolls," the last person tapped will jump up and chase the person who is It around the circle. It will attempt to sit in the vacated seat before being tagged by the person who jumped up. Do you have any questions? Allow kids to play for two or three minutes then form pairs to discuss the following questions:

● **How did you feel while you were playing the game?**
● **Are you interested in the same things now that you were interested in as a child? Why or why not?**
● **What's good about growing up?**
● **What's bad about growing up?**

Ask a volunteer to read Mark 10:13-15. Ask:

● **What do you think Jesus means when he says we must become like children?**
● **What is difficult about following Jesus' instruction to be childlike?**

Give pairs an opportunity to share what they discovered. Then say: **We are maturing physically, emotionally, and spiritually. With that maturity comes new freedom and new power. And with maturity comes new responsibilities and concerns. Jesus never told us to avoid responsibility. Jesus told us to trust him and believe in him even when things are difficult and chaotic. You are a child of God, and you can trust that God is a perfect and loving father.**

BIBLE EXPERIENCES ▼

God the F-A-T-H-E-R (5 to 10 minutes)

Give a pencil and a sheet of paper to each student. Say: **Turn your paper sideways so the long edge is on the bottom. Write "FATHER" in capital letters down the left side of the paper. Take a couple of minutes to think of words that describe what an earthly father is like. Try to come up with at least one word for each letter of the word father. For example, for the letter F you could write the word "fun." Write at least one word that begins with each letter.**

While kids work, write the following Scripture references on a sheet of newsprint, and tape the newsprint to a wall: Psalm 68:4-6; Isaiah 45:18-19; Matthew 7:9-11; and Ephesians 2:4-7.

When kids finish, have them turn their sheets of paper over. Say: **I'd like you to do the same thing on the back side of the paper. Write "FATHER" in capital letters down the left side of the paper, but this time, write words that describe God. Before you begin, I'd like you to read all of the verses on the sheet of newsprint. Use the verses**

DEPTH FINDER

UNDERSTANDING THE BIBLE

In Mark 10:15, Jesus explains that we "must accept the kingdom of God as if (we) were little (children)." But Hebrews 6:1 states that we must "leave the elementary teachings about Christ and go on to maturity" (New International Version). So which is correct? Are we to grapple with the deeper issues of Christianity or simply accept them as a child does?

Jesus never instructed his followers to be foolish, irresponsible, or thoughtless. He instructed them to be receptive to the kingdom of God. As *The Expositor's Bible Commentary* explains from *The Gospel According to St. Mark* by A.E.J. Rawlinson, "children are unself-conscious, receptive, and content to be dependent on others' care and bounty; it is in such a spirit that the kingdom must be 'received'—it is a gift of God, and not an achievement on the part of man; it must be simply accepted, inasmuch as it can never be deserved."

Jesus provided a context for our faith—childlike trust. As children, we are to accept the fact that God knows what he is doing and to trust that his purposes will be accomplished. We are free to grapple with the difficult issues of Christianity within the security of childlike trust in God. We *must* go on in maturity. We *should* ask the difficult questions. But as we seek understanding, we can rest in the fact that God is a loving, just, and holy Father. As we wrestle with the difficulties of Christian faith, we can accept the kingdom of God as children—even when we cannot understand it.

to guide you as you come up with words for each letter. This list may be very similar to the first or it may be very different. When kids are finished, ask:

- **How do your two lists differ?**
- **How are they similar?**
- **What kind of father is God? Explain.**
- **What do you think it means to be a child of God?**

Ask a volunteer to read Romans 8:15-17 aloud. Say: **Sometimes it's difficult to remember or even believe that you are a child  of God.** **Sometimes we have difficulty acting like children of God because we don't trust or know God. God is the perfect Father. As we come to know God and grow in faith, we can live like his children.**

No News Is Good News (20 to 25 minutes)

Have kids form groups of four. Give a pencil and a sheet of paper to each student and a newspaper to each group. Tape a sheet of newsprint to the wall and write these four categories: Death, Sex, Drugs and Alcohol, and Relationships.

Say: **Use your newspapers to find facts or stories about each of these categories. List each category on your paper, then list all the facts or headlines you can find that have something to do with each category. Make it a priority to find one fact or headline about each category, then search for additional facts and headlines for all the categories.**

LEADER TIP

for God the F-A-T-H-E-R

Some students may not have a positive image of fathers. To help kids understand that God is a perfect and loving father, consider asking questions like, "Does your image of earthly fathers make it difficult to relate to God as your father? If so, how?"

LEADER TIP

for No News Is Good News

If you are unable to obtain enough newspapers for this activity, consider using news magazines such as Newsweek or Time.

Give kids about ten minutes to search, then give a "Do I Have to Grow Up?" handout (p. 56) to each group. Ask kids to look at the fact listed in each category on the handout. After a minute, ask:

● **How are the facts and headlines you found in your newspaper like the facts on the handout?**

● **How are they different?**

● **Are you hopeful about the future? Why or why not?**

● **What about our world makes it difficult to live like <u>we are children of God?</u>**

Say: **As we grow up, we lose some of the idealism we had as children. When we see the suffering and sin of the world, we can become hopeless and cynical. God doesn't want us to become hopeless or joyless. God wants us to live in the hope of being his children. Within your group, look up the Scriptures of Hope on your handouts. Under the Scripture, write down what it says about the issue and how it can help you have childlike hope in God.**

After about ten minutes, ask:

● **Have you faced pressures like the ones found in the facts? Explain.**

● **Do you believe the pressure you feel has caused you to grow up too fast? Why or why not?**

● **What hope did you find in the Scriptures?**

● **How can the Scriptures you read help you live out your identity as a child of God?**

● **What are some practical ways we can act on the Scriptures of hope we have read?**

REFLECTION ▼

The Journey (10 to 15 minutes) Give each person a balloon. Have kids stand in a line across one end of the room and write their initials on their balloons with markers. As they work, tape a sheet of paper to the wall on the opposite side of the room and write "God" on the sheet.

Say: **You're going on a journey. Each of you is going to travel from this side of the room to where God is on the other side of the room. To move, you must blow up your balloon, let it go, and walk over to the place where it lands. Continue to do this until you get over to the wall with the sheet marked "God" on it. Are there any questions?**

Have kids begin the journey. After about half of your kids have made it to the wall, say: **Everyone freeze where you are!** Ask:

● **How does it feel to not be able to make it over to God?**

● **What things in our lives and in the world make it difficult for us to go to God?**

Ask a volunteer to read Hebrews 10:19-23 aloud. Ask:

● **What benefits come with being children of God?**

● **What do we have to do in order to get to God?**

● **In what ways has God come to you?**

To help kids live out this lesson, plan a Toy Drive for children in your community. Encourage kids to create posters to announce to the congregation the need for new and like new toys. Have kids obtain large boxes to set up drop-off sites. Once the toys have been collected, have kids attach tags to the toys that say: "You are a child of God, and he loves you very much (Matthew 18:1-4)." Encourage your teenagers to decide where they'd like to focus this outreach. Ask for volunteers to call local schools, women's shelters, or the city government to find outlets for distributing the toys. Help the teenagers be active in carrying out this service project.

Say: **Because of Christ's death and your faith in him, <u>you are a child of God.</u> As God's child, you have direct access to him. You don't need to play games, follow rituals, or pay a price to draw near to your Heavenly Father. Put down your balloons and walk over to the wall marked "God."**

After all the kids come to the wall, have them spread out as much as possible and spend a few minutes in prayer. Encourage them to give thanks that they are God's children and to take advantage of the opportunity to speak directly to their Heavenly Father.

> *"Let the little children come to me. Don't stop them, because the kingdom of God belongs to people who are like these children. I tell you the truth, you must accept the kingdom of God as if you were a little child, or you will never enter it."* **—Mark 10:14-15**

Do I Have to Grow Up?

CATEGORY	FACTS	SCRIPTURES OF HOPE
Death	Every year, of the one million who attempt suicide, approximately 5,000 succeed, making suicide the number two cause of death among teens.	John 10:9-10
Sex	Twelve million teen-agers report being sexually active. Seventy-four percent say they would live with someone before marriage.	1 Corinthians 6:18-20
Drugs and Alcohol	Forty-four percent of high school seniors report having used illicit drugs, among them cocaine, marijuana, and heroin. Eight million admit to using alcohol weekly, and almost half a million have more than five drinks in a row weekly.	Ephesians 4:22-24
Relationships	Every year, more than one million teenagers live in families going through a divorce.	Malachi 4:2, 5-6

(Source for statistics: Focus on the Family Web Site on America Online.)

why ▼ Active and Interactive Learning works with teenagers

Let's Start With the Big Picture

Think back to a major life lesson you've learned.
Got it? Now answer these questions:
● Did you learn your lesson from something you read?
● Did you learn it from something you heard?
● Did you learn it from something you experienced?

If you're like 99 percent of your peers, you answered "yes" only to the third question—you learned your life lesson from something you experienced.

This simple test illustrates the most convincing reason for using active and interactive learning with young people: People learn best through experience. Or to put it even more simply, people learn by doing.

Learning by doing is what active learning is all about. No more sitting quietly in chairs and listening to a speaker expound theories about God—that's passive learning. Active learning gets kids out of their chairs and into the experience of life. With active learning, kids get to *do* what they're studying. They *feel* the effects of the principles you teach. They *learn* by experiencing truth firsthand.

Active learning works because it recognizes three basic learning needs and uses them in concert to enable young people to make discoveries on their own and to find practical life applications for the truths they believe.

So what are these three basic learning needs?
1. Teenagers need action.
2. Teenagers need to think.
3. Teenagers need to talk.

Read on to find out exactly how these needs will be met by using the active and interactive learning techniques in Group's Core Belief Bible Study Series in your youth group.

1. Teenagers Need Action

Aircraft pilots know well the difference between passive and active learning. Their passive learning comes through listening to flight instructors and reading flight-instruction books. Their active learning comes through actually flying an airplane or flight simulator. Books and lectures may be helpful, but pilots really learn to fly by manipulating a plane's controls themselves.

We can help young people learn in a similar way. Though we may engage students passively in some reading and listening to teachers, their understanding and application of God's Word will really take off through simulated and real-life experiences.

Forms of active learning include simulation games; role-plays; service projects; experiments; research projects; group pantomimes; mock trials; construction projects; purposeful games; field trips; and, of course, the most powerful form of active learning—real-life experiences.

We can more fully explain active learning by exploring four of its characteristics:

● **Active learning is an adventure.** Passive learning is almost always predictable. Students sit passively while the teacher or speaker follows a planned outline or script.

In active learning, kids may learn lessons the teacher never envisioned. Because the leader trusts students to help create the learning experience, learners may venture into unforeseen discoveries. And often the teacher learns as much as the students.

● **Active learning is fun and captivating.** What are we communicating when we say, "OK, the fun's over—time to talk about God"? What's the hidden message? That joy is separate from God? And that learning is separate from joy?

What a shame.

Active learning is not joyless. One seventh-grader we interviewed clearly remembered her best Sunday school lesson: "Jesus was the light, and we went into a dark room and shut off the lights. We had a candle, and we learned that Jesus is the light and the dark can't shut off the light." That's active learning. Deena enjoyed the lesson. She had fun. And she learned.

Active learning intrigues people. Whether they find a foot-washing experience captivating or maybe a bit uncomfortable, they learn. And they learn on a level deeper than any work sheet or teacher's lecture could ever reach.

● **Active learning involves everyone.** Here the difference between passive and active learning becomes abundantly clear. It's like the difference between watching a football game on television and actually playing in the game.

The "trust walk" provides a good example of involving everyone in active learning. Half of the group members put on blindfolds; the other half serve as guides. The "blind" people trust the guides to lead them through the building or outdoors. The guides prevent the blind people from falling down stairs or tripping over rocks. Everyone needs to participate to learn the inherent lessons of trust, faith, doubt, fear, confidence, and servanthood. Passive spectators of this experience would learn little, but participants learn a great deal.

● **Active learning is focused through debriefing.** Activity simply for activity's sake doesn't usually result in good learning. Debriefing—evaluating an experience by discussing it in pairs or small groups—helps focus the experience and draw out its meaning. Debriefing helps sort and order the information students gather during the experience. It helps learners relate the recently experienced activity to their lives.

The process of debriefing is best started immediately after an experience. We use a three-step process in debriefing: reflection, interpretation, and application.

Reflection—This first step asks the students, "How did you feel?" Active-learning experiences typically evoke an emotional reaction, so it's appropriate to begin debriefing at that level.

Some people ask, "What do feelings have to do with education?" Feelings have everything to do with education. Think back again to that time in your life when you learned a big lesson. In all likelihood, strong feelings accompanied that lesson. Our emotions tend to cement things into our memories.

When you're debriefing, use open-ended questions to probe feelings. Avoid questions that can be answered with a "yes" or "no." Let your learners know that there are no wrong answers to these "feeling" questions. Everyone's feelings are valid.

Interpretation—The next step in the debriefing process asks, "What does this mean to you? How is this experience like or unlike some other aspect of your life?" Now you're asking people to identify a message or principle from the experience.

You want your learners to discover the message for themselves. So instead of telling students your answers, take the time to ask questions that encourage self-discovery. Use Scripture and discussion in pairs or small groups to explore how the actions and effects of the activity might translate to their lives.

Alert! Some of your people may interpret wonderful messages that you never intended. That's not failure! That's the Holy Spirit at work. God allows us to catch different glimpses of his kingdom even when we all look through the same glass.

Application—The final debriefing step asks, "What will you do about it?" This step moves learning into action. Your young people have shared a common experience. They've discovered a principle. Now they must create something new with what they've just experienced and interpreted. They must integrate the message into their lives.

The application stage of debriefing calls for a decision. Ask your students how they'll change, how they'll grow, what they'll do as a result of your time together.

2. Teenagers Need to Think

Today's students have been trained not to think. They aren't dumber than previous generations. We've simply conditioned them not to use their heads.

You see, we've trained our kids to respond with the simplistic answers they think the teacher wants to hear. Fill-in-the-blank student workbooks and teachers who ask dead-end questions such as "What's the capital of Delaware?" have produced kids and adults who have learned not to think.

And it doesn't just happen in junior high or high school. Our children are schooled very early not to think. Teachers attempt to help kids read with nonsensical fill-in-the-blank drills, word scrambles, and missing-letter puzzles.

Helping teenagers think requires a paradigm shift in how we teach. We need to plan for and set aside time for higher-order thinking and be willing to reduce our time spent on lower-order parroting. Group's Core Belief Bible Study Series is designed to help you do just that.

Thinking classrooms look quite different from traditional classrooms. In most church environments, the teacher does most of the talking and hopes that knowledge will transmit from his or her brain to the students'. In thinking settings, the teacher coaches students to ponder, wonder, imagine, and problem-solve.

3. Teenagers Need to Talk

Everyone knows that the person who learns the most in any class is the teacher. Explaining a concept to someone else is usually more helpful to the explainer than to the listener. So why not let the students do more teaching? That's one of the chief benefits of letting kids do the talking. This process is called interactive learning.

What is interactive learning? Interactive learning occurs when students discuss and work cooperatively in pairs or small groups.

Interactive learning encourages learners to work together. It honors the fact that students can learn from one another, not just from the teacher. Students work together in pairs or small groups to accomplish shared goals. They build together, discuss together, and present together. They teach each other and learn from one another. Success as a group is celebrated. Positive interdependence promotes individual and group learning.

Interactive learning not only helps people learn but also helps learners feel better about themselves and get along better with others. It accomplishes these things more effectively than the independent or competitive methods.

Here's a selection of interactive learning techniques that are used in Group's Core Belief Bible Study Series. With any of these models, leaders may assign students to specific partners or small groups. This will maximize cooperation and learning by preventing all the "rowdies" from linking up. And it will allow for new friendships to form outside of established cliques.

Following any period of partner or small-group work, the leader may reconvene the entire class for large-group processing. During this time the teacher may ask for reports or discoveries from individuals or teams. This technique builds in accountability for the teacherless pairs and small groups.

Pair-Share—With this technique each student turns to a partner and responds to a question or problem from the teacher or leader. Every learner responds. There are no passive observers. The teacher may then ask people to share their partners' responses.

Study Partners—Most curricula and most teachers call for Scripture passages to be read to the whole class by one person. One reads; the others doze.

Why not relinquish some teacher control and let partners read and react with each other? They'll all be involved—and will learn more.

Learning Groups—Students work together in small groups to create a model, design artwork, or study a passage or story; then they discuss what they learned through the experience. Each person in the learning group may be assigned a specific role. Here are some examples:

Reader

Recorder (makes notes of key thoughts expressed during the reading or discussion)

Checker (makes sure everyone understands and agrees with answers arrived at by the group)

Encourager (urges silent members to share their thoughts)

When everyone has a specific responsibility, knows what it is, and contributes to a small group, much is accomplished and much is learned.

Summary Partners—One student reads a paragraph, then the partner summarizes the paragraph or interprets its meaning. Partners alternate roles with each paragraph.

The paraphrasing technique also works well in discussions. Anyone who wishes to share a thought must first paraphrase what the previous person said. This sharpens listening skills and demonstrates the power of feedback communication.

Jigsaw—Each person in a small group examines a different concept, Scripture, or part of an issue. Then each teaches the others in the group. Thus, all members teach, and all must learn the others' discoveries. This technique is called a jigsaw because individuals are responsible to their group for different pieces of the puzzle.

JIGSAW EXAMPLE

Here's an example of a jigsaw.

Assign four-person teams. Have teammates each number off from one to four. Have all the Ones go to one corner of the room, all the Twos to another corner, and so on.

Tell team members they're responsible for learning information in their numbered corners and then for teaching their team members when they return to their original teams.

Give the following assignments to various groups:

Ones: Read Psalm 22. Discuss and list the prophecies made about Jesus.

Twos: Read Isaiah 52:13–53:12. Discuss and list the prophecies made about Jesus.

Threes: Read Matthew 27:1-32. Discuss and list the things that happened to Jesus.

Fours: Read Matthew 27:33-66. Discuss and list the things that happened to Jesus.

After the corner groups meet and discuss, instruct all learners to return to their original teams and report what they've learned. Then have each team determine which prophecies about Jesus were fulfilled in the passages from Matthew.

Call on various individuals in each team to report one or two prophecies that were fulfilled.

You Can Do It Too!

All this information may sound revolutionary to you, but it's really not. God has been using active and interactive learning to teach his people for generations. Just look at Abraham and Isaac, Jacob and Esau, Moses and the Israelites, Ruth and Boaz. And then there's Jesus, who used active learning all the time!

Group's Core Belief Bible Study Series makes it easy for you to use active and interactive learning with your group. The active and interactive elements are automatically built in! Just follow the outlines, and watch as your kids grow through experience and positive interaction with others.

FOR DEEPER STUDY

For more information on incorporating active and interactive learning into your work with teenagers, check out these resources:

● *Why Nobody Learns Much of Anything at Church: And How to Fix It,* by Thom and Joani Schultz (Group Publishing) and
● *Do It! Active Learning in Youth Ministry,* by Thom and Joani Schultz (Group Publishing).
